How's Life Treating You

Consultation on Trauma, Resilience,Healing And Taking Charge of Your Life

Table of Content

Chapter 1: Finding and overcoming your trauma

Emotional and Psychological Trauma

When horrible things happen, it might take a time to get over the trauma and feel secure again. But with these self-help tactics and assistance, you can speed up your recovery.

The young lady on the couch, arms clenched around knees, hand covering lips, nervous.

What is emotional and psychological trauma?

Emotional and psychological trauma is the outcome of exceptionally stressful experiences that destroy your feeling of security, making you feel powerless in a frightening environment. Psychological trauma may leave you battling with uncomfortable feelings, memories, and anxieties that won't go away. It may also leave you feeling numb, distant, and difficult to trust other people.

Traumatic situations frequently include danger to life or safety, but any circumstance that leaves you feeling overwhelmed and alienated may end in trauma, even if it doesn't involve physical injury. It's not the factual conditions that decide whether an incident is traumatic, but your subjective emotional experience of the event. The more afraid and powerless you feel, the more likely you are to be traumatized.

Emotional and psychological trauma may be induced by:

One-time incidents, such as an accident, injury, or a violent assault, particularly if it was unexpected or occurred in infancy.
Ongoing, unrelenting stress, such as living in a crime-ridden area, suffering a life-threatening disease, or enduring traumatic experiences that recur frequently, such as bullying, marital abuse, or childhood mistreatment.
Commonly neglected reasons, such as surgery (particularly in the first 3 years of life), the abrupt loss of someone close, the dissolution of an important relationship, or a humiliating or severely disappointing event, especially if someone was purposefully harsh.

Coping with the trauma of a natural or manufactured catastrophe may provide unique challenges—even if you weren't personally engaged in the event. In reality, although it's exceedingly unlikely any of us will ever be the direct victims of a terrorist attack, aircraft accident, or mass shooting, for example, we're all routinely assaulted with awful photos on social media and news sources of those individuals who have been.

Viewing these sights again and over might overload your nervous system and induce severe stress. Whatever the origin of your trauma, and whether it occurred years ago or yesterday, you may make therapeutic adjustments and go on with your life.

Childhood trauma and the risk of future trauma

While traumatic events may happen to anybody, you're more likely to be traumatized by an incident if you're already under a significant stress load, have recently experienced a series of losses, or have been traumatized before—especially if the previous trauma happened in infancy. Childhood trauma may occur from anything that interrupts a child's feeling of safety, including:

- An unstable or dangerous environment
- Separation from a parent
- Serious sickness
- Intrusive medical treatments
- Sexual, physical, or verbal abuse
- Domestic violence
- Neglect

Experiencing trauma in childhood might result in a severe and long-lasting impact. When childhood trauma is not addressed, a feeling of dread and powerlessness continues over into adulthood, creating the scene for subsequent trauma. However, even if your trauma occurred many years ago, there are measures you can take to overcome the suffering, learn to trust and connect to people again, and reclaim your sense of emotional equilibrium.

Symptoms of psychological trauma
We all respond to trauma in various ways, experiencing a broad spectrum of physical and mental symptoms. There is no "right" or "wrong" way to think, feel, or behave, so don't criticize your own emotions or those of other people. Your answers are NORMAL reactions to ABNORMAL occurrences.

Emotional & psychological symptoms:

- Shock, denial, or disbelief
- Confusion, trouble focusing
- Anger, irritation, mood swings
- Anxiety and fear
- Guilt, shame, self-blame
- Withdrawing from others\sFeeling depressed or hopeless
- Feeling distant or numb

Physical symptoms:
- Insomnia or nightmares
- Fatigue
- Being shocked easily
- Difficulty concentrating
- Racing heartbeat
- Edginess and agitation
- Aches and pains
- Muscle tension
- Healing from trauma

Trauma symptoms often endure from a few days to a few months, gradually dissipating as you absorb the upsetting incident. But even when you're feeling better, you may be bothered from time to time by unpleasant memories or emotions—especially in reaction to triggers such as an anniversary of the occurrence or anything that reminds you of the trauma.

If your psychological trauma symptoms don't lighten up—or if they grow even worse—and you discover that you're unable to move on from the incident for an extended period of time, you may be suffering from Post-Traumatic Stress Disorder (PTSD) (PTSD).

While emotional trauma is a typical reaction to a troubling occurrence, it becomes PTSD when your nervous system becomes "stuck" and you stay in psychological shock, unable to make sense of what occurred or process your feelings.

Whether or whether a traumatic incident includes death, you as a survivor must deal with the loss, at least momentarily, of your feeling of safety. The natural emotion of this loss is mourning. Like others who have lost a loved one, you need to go through a mourning process.

The following techniques may help you deal with the sensation of sadness, recover from the trauma, and go on with your life.

Trauma recovery tip 1: Get moving

Trauma alters your body's natural homeostasis, locking you in a state of hyperarousal and terror. As well as burning off adrenaline and generating endorphins, exercise and movement may assist restore your neurological system.

Try to exercise for 30 minutes or more on most days. Or if it's simpler, three 10-minute bursts of activity every day are just as healthy.

Exercise that is rhythmic and uses both your arms and legs—such as walking, jogging, swimming, basketball, or even dancing—works best.

Add a mindfulness aspect. Instead of concentrating on your thoughts or distracting yourself as you work out, fully concentrate on your body and how it feels as you move. Notice the sensation of your feet striking the ground, for example, or the rhythm of your breathing, or the sense of wind on your skin. Rock climbing, boxing, weight training, or martial arts may make this easier—after all, you need to concentrate on your body motions during these sports to prevent harm.

Tip 2: Don't isolate

Following a trauma, you may want to retreat from people, yet solitude just makes things worse. Connecting to people face to face can help you recover, so make an effort to maintain your connections and avoid spending too much time alone.

You don't have to speak about the trauma. Connecting with people doesn't have to require talking about the trauma. In fact, for some individuals, that might only make matters worse. Comfort comes from feeling involved and accepted by others.

Ask for help. While you don't have to speak about the trauma itself, you must have someone to discuss your experiences with face to face, someone who will listen carefully without judging you. Turn to a trustworthy family member, friend, counselor, or pastor.

Participate in social events, even if you don't feel like it. Do "normal" activities with other people, activities that have nothing to do with the traumatic incident.

Reconnect with old pals. If you've withdrawn from connections that were previously essential to you, make the effort to reconnect.

Join a support group for trauma sufferers. Connecting with people who are suffering the same challenges may help minimize your feeling of isolation, and hearing how others deal can help encourage you in your recovery.

Volunteer. As well as helping others, volunteering may be a terrific way to fight the feeling of powerlessness that frequently follows trauma. Remind yourself of your abilities and restore your feeling of power by helping others.

Make new pals. If you live alone or distant from family and friends, it's crucial to seek out and create new connections. Take a class or join a club to meet others with similar interests, connect to an alumni organization, or reach out to neighbors or work colleagues.

If connecting to people is difficult…
Many individuals who have suffered trauma feel alienated, and withdrawn and find it difficult to connect with other people. If that describes you, there are certain activities you may do before you next meet with a friend:

Exercise or motion. Jump up and down, swing your arms and legs, or simply flail about. Your brain will feel clearer and you'll find it simpler to connect.

Vocal toning. As weird as it seems, voice toning is a terrific method to open up to social contact. Sit up straight and just make "mmmm" noises. Change the pitch and loudness until you sense a nice vibration on your face.

Tip 3: Self-regulate your neurological system

No matter how angry, worried, or out of control you feel, it's crucial to realize that you can modify your arousal system and calm yourself. Not only will it help ease the anxiety associated with trauma, but it will also inspire a stronger feeling of control.

Mindful breathing. If you are feeling bewildered, confused, or agitated, practicing mindful breathing is a simple approach to calm yourself. Simply take 60 breaths, concentrating your attention on each 'out-breath.

Sensory input. Does a certain sight, scent, or flavor rapidly make you feel calm? Or maybe caressing an animal or listening to music serves to fast settle you? Everyone reacts to sensory input a little differently, so try various rapid stress reduction tactics to discover what works best for you.

Staying grounded. To feel in the present and more grounded, sit on a chair. Feel your feet on the ground and your back against the chair. Look around you and identify six items that have red or blue in them. Notice how your breathing grows deeper and calmer.

Allow yourself to experience what you feel when you feel it. Acknowledge your emotions regarding the trauma as they come and accept them. HelpGuide's Emotional Intelligence Toolkit may assist.

Tip 4: Take care of your health

It's true: having a healthy physique may boost your capacity to deal with the stress of trauma.

Get lots of sleep. After a stressful encounter, anxiety or dread may alter your sleep habits. But a lack of quality sleep might increase your trauma symptoms and make it difficult to maintain your emotional equilibrium. Go to sleep and get up at the same time each day and strive for 7 to 9 hours of sleep each night.

Avoid drinking and drugs. Their usage may intensify your trauma symptoms and cause feelings of melancholy, anxiety, and isolation.

Eat a well-balanced diet. Eating modest, well-balanced meals throughout the day can help you keep your energy up and reduce mood fluctuations. Avoid sugary and fried meals and consume enough omega-3 fats—such as salmon, walnuts, soybeans, and flaxseeds—to give your mood a boost.

Reduce stress. Try relaxing methods such as meditation, yoga, or deep breathing exercises. Schedule time for things that offer you delight such as your favorite hobbies.

When to seek professional counseling for trauma

Recovering from trauma takes time, and everyone recovers at their rate. But if months have passed and your symptoms aren't easing up, you may need professional therapy from a trauma specialist.

Seek therapy for trauma if you're:

Having problems functioning at home or work

Suffering from acute dread, anxiety, or sadness

Unable to develop intimate, rewarding connections

Experiencing horrific recollections, nightmares, or flashbacks

Avoiding more and more everything that reminds you of the trauma

Emotionally numb and distant from others

Using drinks or drugs to feel better

Working through trauma may be dangerous, difficult, and sometimes re-traumatizing, therefore this healing process is best completed with the guidance of an experienced trauma expert. Finding the proper therapist may take some time. The therapist you pick must have expertise in treating trauma. But the quality of the interaction with your therapist is as crucial. Choose a trauma expert you are comfortable with. If you don't feel comfortable, respected, or understood, find another therapist.

Ask yourself:
Did you feel comfortable expressing your difficulties with the therapist?
Did you feel like the therapist understood what you were talking about?
Were your concerns handled seriously or were they downplayed or dismissed?
Were you handled with compassion and respect?

Do you suppose that you could develop to trust the therapist?

Treatment for trauma

To recover from psychological and emotional trauma, you'll need to resolve the unpleasant sensations and memories you've long avoided, release pent-up "fight-or-flight" energy, learn to manage powerful emotions, and regain your capacity to trust other people. A trauma expert may employ a range of different therapeutic techniques in your treatment.

The somatic experience focuses on body sensations, rather than ideas and recollections regarding the traumatic incident. By focussing on what's occurring in your body, you may release pent-up trauma-related energy via shaking, weeping, and other types of physical release.

Cognitive-behavioral therapy helps you analyze and assess your ideas and emotions regarding a trauma.

EMDR (Eye Movement Desensitization and Reprocessing) mixes components of cognitive-behavioral therapy with eye movements or other types of rhythmic, left-right stimulation that help "unfreeze" painful memories.

Helping a loved one cope with trauma
When a loved one has undergone trauma, your support may play a significant part in their rehabilitation.

Be patient and understanding. Healing from trauma takes time. Be patient with the rate of rehabilitation and realize that everyone's reaction to trauma is different. Don't evaluate your loved one's reaction against your response or anybody else's.

Offer practical assistance to help your loved one get back into a routine. That may involve assisting with getting groceries or doing cleaning, for example, or just being ready to speak or listen.

Don't rush your loved ones into talking but be accessible if they want to chat. Some trauma survivors find it difficult to speak about what occurred. Don't push your loved ones to open up but let them know you are there to listen if they want to chat, or available to simply hang out if they don't.

Help your loved one to mingle and unwind. Encourage them to engage in physical activity, seek out friends, and pursue hobbies and other things that offer them joy. Take a fitness class together or establish a regular lunch appointment with pals.

Don't take the trauma symptoms personally. Your loved one may become angry, impatient, withdrawn, or emotionally distant. Remember that this is a product of the trauma and may not have anything to do with you or your relationship.

To assist a youngster heal from trauma, it's crucial to talk honestly. Let them know that it's natural to feel terrified or unhappy. Your kid may also look to you for indications on how they should react to trauma, so let them witness you healthily coping with your symptoms.

How children respond to emotional and psychological stress
Some frequent responses to trauma and techniques to help your kid cope with them:

Regression. Many youngsters need to return to an earlier period when they felt safer. Younger children may wet the bed or desire a bottle; older children may dread being alone. It's crucial to be empathetic, patient, and reassuring if your kid reacts this way.

Thinking the incident is their fault. Children younger than 8 tend to assume that if anything goes wrong, it must be their fault. Be sure your youngster knows that he or she did not cause the tragedy.

Sleep problems. Some youngsters have difficulties falling asleep; others wake often or have unpleasant nightmares. Give your youngster a plush animal, warm blanket, or flashlight to take to bed. Try spending additional time together in the evening, enjoying calm hobbies like reading. Be patient. It may take a long before your kid can sleep through the night again.

Feeling helpless. Being engaged in a campaign to prevent an incident from occurring again, sending thank you notes to individuals who have helped, and caring for others may offer a feeling of optimism and control to everyone in the family.

How to Cope with Traumatic Events

Any traumatic event—from a personal tragedy to a global crisis—can take an emotional toll and induce severe stress. But there are methods to retake control of your life.

Man in sorrow, forehead resting on folded hands, partner beside him, reassuring him

The emotional reaction to terrible occurrences

It's typical to suffer traumatic stress after a troubling occurrence, whether it's a traffic accident, aircraft crash, violent crime, terrorist attack, a worldwide epidemic, or a natural catastrophe like an earthquake, storm, or flood. You may experience extreme shock, uncertainty, and terror, or feel numb or overwhelmed by a multitude of contradicting feelings, sometimes all at once. And these feelings aren't confined to the folks who experienced the incident. Round-the-clock news and social media coverage mean that we're all assaulted with awful pictures of disaster, pain, and loss nearly the minute they occur anywhere around the globe. Repeated exposure may overload your nervous system and generate severe stress just as if you experienced the incident personally.

Traumatic stress may destroy your sense of security, leaving you feeling powerless and unprotected in a hazardous world—especially if the traumatic event was created, such as a shooting or act of terrorism. You may feel physically and emotionally fatigued, overtaken with sadness, or find it difficult to concentrate, sleep, or manage your anger. These are all natural reactions to abnormal occurrences.

Often, the uncomfortable thoughts and sensations of traumatic stress—as well as any unpleasant physical symptoms—start to disappear as life gradually returns to normal during the days or weeks after a tragic incident or crisis. But there's also a lot you can do to aid in your recovery and better come to terms with the trauma you've encountered. Whether you lived through the incident directly, observed it, were an emergency responder or medical professional, or suffered severe stress in the aftermath, there are many strategies to quiet your nervous system and recover your emotional equilibrium.

Signs and symptoms of traumatic stress
Whether or not the traumatic incident directly harmed you, it's common to feel apprehensive, terrified, and confused about what the future may contain. Your

neurological system has been overloaded by stress, causing a broad variety of powerful emotions and physical responses. These symptoms of traumatic stress may vary from moderate to severe and typically come and go in waves. There may be moments when you feel jumpy and worried, for example, and other times when you feel detached and numb.

Emotional signs of traumatic stress include:\sShock and disbelief. You have a hard time embracing the reality of what occurred, or feel numb and removed from your emotions.

Fear. You fear that the same event may happen again, or that you'll lose control or break down.

Sadness or sadness, particularly if individuals you know died or had life-altering repercussions.

Helplessness. The rapid, unexpected nature of violent crime, accidents, pandemics, or natural catastrophes may leave you feeling vulnerable and powerless and can induce anxiety or despair.

Guilt because you lived while others died, or feeling that you could have done more to assist.

Anger. You may be furious with God, governments, or those you believe are responsible or be prone to emotional outbursts.

Shame, particularly over sentiments or concerns that you can't control.

Relief. You may feel pleased that the worst is past, that you weren't as seriously impacted as others, or even optimistic that your life will return to normal.

Physical symptoms include:

Feeling dizzy or faint, stomach clenching or churning, heavy perspiration.

Trembling, shaking, experiencing cold chills, having a lump in your throat, or feeling choked up.

Rapid breathing, beating heart, even chest aches, or trouble breathing.

Racing thoughts, being unable to relax or stop pacing. You may also have difficulties focusing, memory issues, or confusion.

Changes in your sleeping habits. You endure sleeplessness or nightmares, for example.

Unexplained aches and pains, including headaches, and changes in sexual function.

Loss or increase in appetite, or excessive use of alcohol, nicotine, or narcotics.

What's the difference between traumatic stress and PTSD?

While the symptoms of traumatic stress and post-traumatic stress disorder (PTSD) seem quite similar immediately after a tragedy or unsettling incident, they proceed very differently. As unpleasant as the symptoms of traumatic stress might be, they tend to progressively improve with time, particularly if you take efforts to care for your mental health.

However, if your traumatic stress symptoms don't clear up and your nervous system stays "stuck," unable to move on from the experience for a longer period, you may be having PTSD.

With PTSD, you stay in psychological shock. The symptoms don't lessen and you don't feel a bit better each day. You may even start to feel worse.

Witnessing tragedy and suffering, making life-and-death choices, and even putting yourself in harm's way, may take a toll on your mental health and induce catastrophic stress. And because you may have to regularly cope with the consequences of terrible incidents throughout your work, the emotional damage might grow over time. If the stress is left uncontrolled, it may develop into burnout, a condition of emotional, mental, and physical weariness.

It's crucial to remember that taking care of your own needs is not selfish, especially during a moment of crisis. Rather, it's a requirement. After all, by allowing yourself to take pauses, depending on people for support, and working in teams rather than alone for lengthy periods, you'll have the energy and grit to better aid those in need.

Traumatic stress red flags include:

It's been six weeks, and you're not feeling any better.
You've had problems functioning at home and work.
You're having horrific recollections, nightmares, or flashbacks.
You're having an increasingly difficult time connecting and relating to people.

You're suffering suicidal thoughts or emotions.
You're avoiding more and more items that remind you of a tragedy or terrible occurrence.

If your kid has been traumatized …
The powerful, perplexing, and terrifying feelings that accompany a tragic incident may be much more prominent in

children—whether they actually experienced the event or were frequently exposed to distressing media coverage. But you can assist your kid deal with emotional stress and move on from the incident

Chapter 2: Resilience

Resilience refers to both the process and the product of effectively adjusting to harsh or challenging life circumstances, according to the definition from the American Psychological Association (APA) (APA). It's having the mental, emotional, and behavioral flexibility and capacity to respond to both internal and external challenges, according to APA.

"You can resist adversity and bounce back and thrive despite life's downturns," says Amit Sood, MD, the executive director of the Global Center for Resiliency and Well-Being and the inventor of the Resilient Option program.

What Is Resilience?

Resilience is the capacity to deal with and recover from adversity. People who stay calm amid calamity have resilience. People with psychological resilience can utilize their abilities and strengths to react to life's obstacles, which might include those connected to:

- Death of a loved one
- Divorce
- Financial concerns
- Illness
- Job loss
- Medical emergencies
- Natural catastrophes

Instead of slipping into despair or fleeing from troubles by utilizing unhealthy coping techniques, resilient individuals tackle life's obstacles head-on.

People with resilience do not endure less pain, sadness, or anxiety than other people do. Instead, they employ healthy coping strategies to face such hardships in ways that nurture strength and development, frequently emerging stronger than they were before.

This article addresses the indications, characteristics, and causes of resilience. It also outlines some of the tactics that individuals may employ to become more resilient.

Signs of Resilience

Resilient individuals typically have a lot of distinct attributes that help them weather life's trials. Some of the indications of resilience include:

A survivor mentality: When individuals are resilient, they perceive themselves as survivors. They know that even when things are challenging, they can keep going until they make it through.

Effective emotional regulation: Resilience is characterized by a capacity to control emotions in the face of stress.
This doesn't imply that resilient individuals don't feel intense emotions such as anger, grief, or fear. It signifies that they realize such sentiments are transient and can be handled till they pass.

Feeling in control: Resilient individuals tend to have a strong internal locus of control and believe that their actions may play a role in shaping the fate of events.

Problem-solving skills: When challenges happen, resilient individuals look at the situation objectively and strive to come up with solutions that will make a difference.

Self-compassion: Another hallmark of resilience is exhibiting self-acceptance and self-compassion. Resilient individuals treat themselves with compassion, particularly when circumstances are rough.

Social support: Having a robust network of supporting individuals is another evidence of resilience. Resilient individuals appreciate the need for assistance and recognize when they need to seek help.

Types of Resilience

Resilience shows a capacity to withstand life's adversities and is an overall indication of adaptation. However, there are also several kinds of resilience, each of which might impact a person's capacity to deal with various sorts of stress.

Physical Resilience

Physical resilience relates to how the body copes with change and rebounds from physical challenges, diseases, and injuries. Research shows that this form of resilience plays a significant role in health. It influences how individuals age as well as how they adapt and recover from physical stress and medical disorders.

Physical resilience is something that individuals may improve to a certain extent by adopting good lifestyle choices. Getting adequate sleep, eating a good diet, and participating in regular exercise are just a few methods to improve this form of resilience.

Mental Resilience

Mental resilience refers to a person's capacity to adapt to change and uncertainty. People who exhibit this form of resilience are adaptable and calm during times of stress. They employ mental power to overcome difficulties, move ahead, and stay positive even when they are suffering setbacks.

Emotional Resilience

Emotional resilience is the ability to manage emotions during times of stress. Resilient individuals are conscious of their emotional responses and tend to be in touch with their inner lives. Because of this, they are also able to quiet their thoughts and control their emotions when they are coping with unfavorable circumstances.

This form of resilience also helps individuals keep a feeling of optimism when things are challenging. Because they are emotionally resilient, they recognize that hardship and negative feelings won't continue forever.

Social Resilience

Social resilience, which may also be termed community resilience, is the capacity of groups to rebound from harsh events. It includes individuals engaging with others and working together to address issues that impact people both personally and collectively.

Aspects of social resilience include getting together after catastrophes, helping each other socially, being aware of the hazards that the community confronts, and developing a feeling of community.

Such actions may be critical amid problems such as natural catastrophes that impact communities or large groups of individuals.

Causes of Resilience

Some individuals are innately resilient, possessing personality attributes that enable them to stay unflappable in the face of difficulty.

However, these behaviors are not merely inborn qualities observed in a select few. Resilience is the outcome of a complex combination of internal and environmental qualities, including genetics, physical fitness, mental health, and environment.

Social support is another crucial aspect that leads to resilience. Mentally strong individuals tend to have the support of family and friends to assist build them up in times of adversity.

Resilient persons are also likely to have features like:

- Being an excellent communicator
- Having an internal center of the control
- Having strong emotional intelligence and regulating emotions efficiently
- Holding favorable ideas of oneself and their talents
- Possessing the aptitude to establish realistic plans and stick to them
- Viewing oneself as warriors rather than victims of fate.

Impact of Resilience

Resilience is what provides humans the psychological power to deal with adversity and misfortune.

It is the mental reservoir of strength that individuals can rely on in times of need to bring them through without breaking apart. Psychologists feel that resilient people are better equipped to withstand adversity and reconstruct their life after a challenge.

Dealing with change or loss is an unavoidable aspect of life. At some time, everyone faces varying degrees of setbacks. Some of these problems could be quite modest (not getting into a class or being turned down for a promotion at work), while others are devastating on a much wider scale (hurricanes and terrorist strikes) (hurricanes and terrorist attacks).

Those who lack resilience may get overwhelmed by such situations. They may focus on difficulties and use ineffective coping techniques to cope with them.

Disappointment or failure could push individuals to unhealthy, harmful, or even hazardous habits. These people are longer to recover from failures and may suffer greater psychological discomfort as a consequence.

How individuals cope with these challenges may have a big effect on not only the immediate result but also the long-term psychological implications.

Resilience does not alleviate stress or erase life's hardships.

People who possess this characteristic don't view life through rose-colored spectacles. They recognize that failures happen and that sometimes life is hard. They still experience the bad emotions that occur after a disaster, but their mental attitude helps them to work through these sensations and heal.

Resilience offers individuals the fortitude to confront issues head-on, overcome hardship, and move on with their life. In the aftermath of large-scale catastrophes such as terrorist attacks, natural disasters, and the COVID-19 pandemic, many people displayed the behaviors that typify resilience—and they suffered fewer symptoms of sadness as a consequence.

Even in the face of tragedies that seem unfathomable, resilience permits individuals to summon the power to not only survive but to flourish.

How to Become More Resilient

Fortunately, resilience is something that individuals can cultivate in themselves. Parents may also assist their children to become resilient. Various processes may lead to better resilience.

Reframe Negative Thoughts

Resilient individuals can look at unpleasant events rationally, but in a manner that doesn't rely on blaming or obsessing over what cannot be altered. Instead of perceiving hardship as overwhelming, reframe thinking to search for little methods to approach the situation and make adjustments that will assist.

Focusing on the positive things you can accomplish is a terrific strategy to move out of a negative mentality.

This strategy may also be utilized to assist youngsters to learn how to better deal with obstacles. Encourage them to think about obstacles in more positive, optimistic ways. In this manner, instead of becoming locked in a cycle of negative feelings, a youngster may learn to perceive these occurrences as chances to push themselves and gain new talents.

Seek Support

Talking about life's challenges doesn't make them go away, but talking with a sympathetic friend or loved one may help individuals feel like they have someone in their corner. That can assist the development of resilience. Discussing things with others may also help individuals get insight into the issues they are encountering, or perhaps come up with fresh solutions for handling them.

To assist a kid to create a support network, parents can attempt to model strong social skills like sharing emotions, being empathic, collaborating with and helping others, and expressing gratitude—and remember to encourage a child's good conduct.

Focus On What Is Within Control

When confronted with a crisis or difficulty, it may be easy to become overwhelmed by situations that seem far beyond our control. Instead of wishing there was some way to go back in time or alter things, it might be good to try concentrating on what we can directly affect. Adults may also assist children to acquire this ability by talking about their circumstances and helping them form a strategy for how they can behave.

Even when the situation looks bad, adopting practical efforts might help improve it. No matter how little these measures may be, they may boost your feeling of control and resilience.

Manage Stress

Building appropriate stress management behaviors is an excellent method to build overall resilience. These habits might include activities that assist general health, including obtaining adequate sleep and exercise, as well as particular acts to take during situations of stress, such:

Progressive muscular relaxation
With sufficient work, adults and children alike may acquire and perfect these talents. Eventually, individuals then tend to feel equipped to tackle stressful events and resilient enough to bounce back swiftly. For individuals battling to keep stress levels under control, it may be good to explore enlisting the expertise of a cognitive therapist.

What are the major components of resilience?

There are a lot of distinct aspects that play a crucial part in resilience. These include coping skills, emotional regulation, a feeling of control, communication skills, and social support. These talents interact to enable individuals to feel confident in their capacity to cope, establish realistic plans to deal with issues, control emotional reactions in the face of stress, and seek out the support and aid they need in times of crisis.

How does trauma influence resilience?

The effect of trauma may depend on a range of variables including a person's age, current resources, and the type of the trauma. People who have excellent support and existing emotional resources are typically likely to emerge from trauma with an even stronger feeling of resilience. Children are frequently resilient to stress, but persistent or cumulative traumas may greatly influence a child's capacity to heal and may impact future resilience.

Chapter 3: Healing

What we give represents useful information from the areas of life most crucial for our own progress.

Be conscious of who you are–your values, limits; wants, and aspirations.

Understand your emotions and learn how to react to them. Consciously.

It always takes two individuals to produce stormy waves in a relationship. One occasionally is enough to save it.

Keep an independent mind to make your own conclusions. Your life is your duty.

Compromise but do not give yourself. Not for love, another person, or a cause. It is unlikely to make anybody pleased.
Stick to what's essential to you, and let the rest go.

Trying to alter people simply creates difficulties in relationships. Focus on developing yourself instead.

At the center of all relationships is the connection to oneself.
Love is not enough. Each intimate connection is a purposeful, constant, and unrestrained investment.

Appreciate your loyal buddy. She loves you for who you are staying by your side in pleasure and in tragedy.

Inside your furious, domineering, and judgmental mother dwells an unloved child–disconnected and lonely. Desperate for connection and compassion.
Ask for aid when you need it. Fighting issues on your own may convert struggle into pain.

Reach out to people. Be the one who keeps a relationship alive.
Take care of your body, it's the home to your spirit.
Make a habit of being kind, giving, and caring. Leave the judgment to disturbed individuals.

Take care of your mental wellness. Turn down on tension. Turn up on positivism.
Feeling indifferent regarding a tough individual is natural. Acknowledge your

emotions, behave according to your ideals, and let go.

Worrying can't alter the past, fix any issue or shield you from unpleasant things in the future. But it may make you unwell.

Don't strive to be flawless. Your weaknesses make you distinct.

Strive to retain balance in everything. Avoid extremes at any expense.

When a boulder blocks your route, be cool. Panicking hinders you from thinking rationally. Use helicopter viewpoint. Observe and learn before making a choice.

You are accountable for your own pleasure. But not for the enjoyment of others.

Change is only possible when you are ready to welcome it.

Look at life through a lens of humor–it not only makes life simpler. It can also save you.

Appreciate what you already have. Turn a gratitude switch on.
Nobody can make you happy since happiness can only be discovered inside.
Making choices, don't overthink. Better to commit errors than later regret missing possibilities.

You have the right to feel sad and to feel furious.
Know and protect your limits. Learn how to say no. Also to your children (start while they are tiny) (start when they are small).

Turn off your autopilot to live mindfully. Life occurs here and now.

Make friends with your inner critic.

Talk less, listen more.
Don't allow anybody to dominate you—not your parents, employer, lover, or your kid.
Treat your relationship like a fruit tree—give it love, patience, lots of nutrients, and a good fertilizer.
Enjoy the harvest.

Chapter 4: Take Charge of Your Life

An experience like you are not in command of your own life is an unnerving feeling. Worse still, many people are not even conscious that they are behaving according to the scripts put out for them by society, family, and other outside influences, without any actual self-direction.

"If your ship doesn't come in, swim out to it." -Jonathan

Are you content with your life?
Do you identify the gnawing sense of not being content in your life? Even when you

are pleased, you may still have the impression that there is more in life.

Happiness is a short-term experience while fulfillment is about your complete life. I would want to provide you with some thoughts on how you might become more fulfilled. The most critical component I have kept for last.

Be thankful
When you search for fulfillment in material things, you will never be fulfilled. There will always be finer goods to purchase. And if you have lovely goods, you will learn that they do not provide you with much happiness. A lot of things also equals a lot of concerns. Things become damaged, they may get lost or stolen.

Practice thankfulness.

Take a daily moment to jot down what you may be thankful for. It might be people around you, accomplishments you are proud of, or an event you have experienced. Think about it and write down why you are glad.

Also, take a look at all the goods you own. Regularly get rid of goods you no longer need. This may also provide tranquility and pleasure. Postpone purchasing stuff that you do not need.

Grow your patience

Our culture is increasingly focused on achieving immediate outcomes. Because of this, we are growing less and less patient. But many areas of life require time. Therefore, you should also plan for breaks for yourself. It enables you to take a distance from the everyday hustle. Go for a stroll in nature or spend time with your family and friends. It will provide you with tranquility and enables you to develop patience.

Do not compare yourself with others
When you compare yourself with others, you rapidly develop the idea that you are not as excellent as them. But not everyone is the same and every individual has their distinct features. By comparing yourself with others all the time, you frequently miss discovering what you may be excellent at. You will get uneasy and unhappy.

Be proud of the things you are excellent at.
If you can't mention any aspects of yourself that you are excellent at, write a

list of 5 examples. Write out 5 areas in which you are superior to individuals you know. Or ask someone you can trust to list a couple of your greatest attributes.

Nurture your connection and your friends
You don't have to be friends with everyone. If you have a partner, spend your time and attention in your relationship. If a relationship lasts for a longer time, the habit might sneak in. Surprise the other person now and again with something kind. Show that you appreciate and respect your spouse.

Also, invest in excellent friends.
Spend time with them often and show interest in what they believe is important.

Accept that your spouse and your pals are different from you. Appreciate their lovely characteristics, but also be mindful that no one is flawless. And here too, don't compare yourself with others. You have your strengths.

Do not keep a grudge
Painful decisions done in the past might haunt you for the rest of your life. They will continue to impact your life if you cannot put them behind. Don't keep grudges or animosity towards other individuals. Try to forgive people who have injured you, even if they are not contrite yet. A resentment may eat you up within.

Be honest
If you are honest with people, you have nothing to conceal. If you are honest, you don't have to twist and turn. It avoids a lot of tough situations. The truth nearly

always comes out. And when it occurs, there is a strong possibility that vital friendships will be lost.

Try an alternative approach
Sometimes you become locked in rigid patterns. You may have done things the same way for many years. If it does not give you a satisfying sensation, take a step back and evaluate what may be altered. Sometimes this might produce emotions of anxiety and uncertainty, but if you do take steps, it can be incredibly satisfying.

Life is not always easy.
For example, you may lose your job. Try to regard these conditions as a fresh chance. Don't become caught in the past, but explore for imaginative new chances.

What is your life purpose?
To be fully fulfilled with your life, you need to understand your mission. After all, if you do not have a purpose, you do not know your goal.

To uncover your life's mission, you will have to look for it. It is necessary to spend time on it. When you know your mission, it will offer you a great sense of calm and happiness.

Bonus Point:

Aim High and Tune Out the Naysayers

People love to throw walls up telling us "you can't", "that's not the way it's done", "no" and other similar mantras of doom and general dead ends.

Often, this boils down to their concerns or beliefs voiced out loud. Maybe they "can't" because they convince themselves they can't. You don't have to engage in it. You may blaze your route instead.

Just because someone says it can't be done, it doesn't always imply it can't be done.

Set your aim high, work hard to reach your aspirations, and fulfill your objectives and you just may surprise yourself (as well as the doubters) (as well as the naysayers). Get accustomed to the reality that you'll hear "you can't" a lot if you attempt just about everything in life. Sometimes you simply have to go ahead and do it anyhow.

Keep your determination firm and focused on what's essential to you.

These suggestions are merely touching the surface of ways that we may all take responsibility for our lives. Add your thoughts and live the life you want, in the manner that you want, and you'll be taking command.

Conclusion

Taking responsibility for your life begins with taking an honest evaluation of where you are at the current time, determining what needs to change and developing objectives that will move the needle.

While this post largely concentrated on producing a change in the area of the profession, the same tactics may be utilized to address any aspect of your life. Stepping up and taking control is the only way to lead yourself to the job and life of your desires.